T5-BQB-639

Keeping Lent, Triduum and Eastertime

Liturgy Training Publications

Acknowledgments

The English translation of the Triduum acclamation from *Rite of Holy Week* © 1972, International Committee on English in the Liturgy, Inc. (ICEL); the English translation of the *Salve Regina* and *Regina Coeli* from *A Book of Prayers* © 1982, ICEL; the English translation of psalms and gospel canticles from the *Liturgical Psalter* © 1994, ICEL. All rights reserved.

Hymns for Lent translated by Peter Scagnelli.

This book was written by Peter Mazar and illustrated by Helen Siegl. It was edited by David Philippart with assistance from Pedro A. Vélez and Theresa Houston. It was designed by Anna Manhart and typeset in Galliard by Karen Mitchell. *Keeping Lent, Triduum and Eastertime* was printed by Salsedo Press of Chicago, Illinois.

Library of Congress Catalog Card Number 96-77207
ISBN 1-56854-033-7

KLTE2

 ® 601

CONTENTS

INTRODUCTION

There are 40 days of Lent, 3 days of Triduum and 50 days of Eastertime.

These days are a single season, the paschal season, the springtime of the church. "Paschal" comes from *Pascha,* passover. Throughout these days we lay aside business-as-usual to keep our Pascha.

In the passover from winter into spring we recognize an image of our own passover in baptism. What was cold becomes warm. What was dark is enlightened. The enslaved are set free, and the dead are raised to life. Throughout the paschal season we return to our baptism, to the death we died in those waters and to the life we gained in the Holy Spirit. We renew our baptismal promises, and we accompany others making those promises for the first time — the catechumens.

Here is a prayerbook for our keeping of the paschal season. Here are prayers and psalms, disciplines and traditions with which the church, all the holy people of God, observe Lent, Triduum and Eastertime.

Take some time to look over this booklet. Decide which disciplines you and your household will embrace, which traditions you will make your own, when and where you will keep the habit of daily prayers. Don't be afraid of repetition, especially when praying the psalms. Repetition is how we learn the psalms by heart, how traditions become a gift to the next generation and how discipline forms us as disciples.

To a good fast! To a glad feast! To a holy Pascha!

CARNIVAL

The days before Ash Wednesday are Carnival time, a high-stepping, high-calorie antidote to winter. It's a time to dance, attend plays, sing around the piano and make merry! Carnival means "farewell to meat," when we say goodbye to feasting and clean the treats out of our cupboards to prepare for lenten fasting. If we take Lent seriously, we naturally take Carnival a bit frivolously. It gets us ready to keep a good Lent.

Invite everyone to a Mardi Gras masquerade on the "fat Tuesday" before Ash Wednesday. Master an ethnic tradition of the season, from puppetry to pantomime, from the polka to the samba. Turn your Carnival celebration into a feast of open-door hospitality. Gather friends and enemies, strangers and the all-too-familiar for a final fling before lenten fasting.

Wearing costumes can be a symbol of heaven, where everything of earth is turned upside down, where fools are wise, the poor are rich, and commoners are kings and queens. Removing our costumes also can be a symbol of heaven, where nothing of earth will be hidden, where honesty and truth will set us free. At midnight on Mardi Gras remove your masks, wipe off your greasepaint and welcome Lent, the season when we see each other as we truly are.

LENT
THE FORTY DAYS

The word "Lent" means springtime. This word comes from the same root as "lengthen," since daytime lengthens during Lent. The Northern Hemisphere turns toward the sun, the source of life, and winter turns into spring. In Hebrew the word for repentance is "to turn," like the turning of the earth to the sun, like the turning of soil before planting.

"Even now, says the Lord, turn to me" (Joel 2:12). The word "sin" means separation. We are called to turn from our separate selves, from our sin, to come together in community. Self-denial is the way we express our repentance. We turn away from sin and death. In the lengthening brightness from Ash Wednesday until Holy Thursday afternoon, our holy Lent, we turn to God as our source of life.

Prayer, Fasting, Almsgiving

Self-denial is threefold, advises chapter six of the Gospel of Matthew. We *pray:* "Go to your room, close your door, and pray to your Father in private." We *fast:* "No one must see you are fasting but your Father." We give alms: "Keep your deeds of mercy secret, and your Father who sees in secret will repay you." Self-denial is an exercise, workout, a getting into shape. Through the lenten exercise of prayer, fasting and almsgiving, we spring clean our lives, sharpen our senses, put tomorrow in its place and treasure the day at hand.

All of us can think of reasons not to pray, fast or give alms. These practices seem old-fashioned, even holier-than-thou. Besides, didn't we get rid of most of the rules about lenten discipline? Yet these rules were relaxed to make these things free gifts we give to one another. In prayer, fasting and works of mercy, we pattern ourselves after the Lord Jesus. Jesus prayed and taught us how to pray. Jesus fasted, and we do likewise. Jesus gave alms (in Hebrew, *tzedakah,* "acts of justice"). And we are asked to give our very lives for each other.

Prayer

Lent is a season of needs, of emptiness, of limitation. Lenten prayer rises out of our weakness, our needs. Only when we realize our emptiness and know that we have limitations can lenten prayer begin. The pages of this book contain simple morning, evening and night prayers: psalms and hymns, the reading of scripture, time for our own words and time for silence. Prayer is a habit. We reserve time each day for it, the best time we can afford.

Whatever else we pray, we begin by tracing the sign of the cross on our bodies. It is a sign of defeat and a sign of victory. For the cross, which marked us at baptism, continues to mark our lives as we struggle in our weakness, as we yearn for the victory of charity and justice.

Fasting

Fasting is specially associated with Lent. Foodstores are at their lowest in earliest spring. Animals are calving or laying eggs. Lenten fasting has its origins in these rhythms of nature. For 40 days we remind ourselves that the earth is like Noah's ark, all creatures gravely dependent on each other. Only by fasting together can we preserve each other's lives, as well as the lives of generations yet to be born.

Saint John Chrysostom called fasting a "medicine," something that makes people healthy. Lenten hunger makes people healthy, purifying our bodies, limiting our consumption of the world's resources, generating less waste, allowing silence and restraint to replace gratification. Fasting also entails less sleep, less speech, less entertainment, so that the discipline of Lent may purify our minds as well as our bodies.

Almsgiving

All year long we tolerate the intolerable: people left hungry, without visitors, without homes. Yet baptism demands our intolerance of evil. As we approach the waters of Easter baptism, the stark honesty of the lenten scriptures challenges us to renew our year-long efforts in the Christian habit of almsgiving. We are invited to give our time, our money and our imaginative efforts to feed the hungry, visit the lonely, and restore dignity and justice to lives warped by human evil. Most specially, almsgiving involves our energy to change systems that murder and torture and oppress people. The gospels are rich in examples of the craftiness and persistence required of every Christian in the pursuit of justice.

Saint Augustine said that prayer requires two wings to fly: fasting and almsgiving. The details are left to our ingenuity and our traditions. We must discuss and decide these details as individuals, as families, as parishes. Alexander Schmemann offers us these criteria: "Let it be limited and humble but consistent and serious." Prayer, fasting and almsgiving are the necessary first course in the banquet of God's reign.

The Forty-Day Journey

It took 40 days for sinfulness to drown under the flood before a new creation could inherit the earth (Genesis 7:4). It took 40 years for the generation of slaves to die before the freeborn could enter the promised land (Numbers 14:33–35). For 40 days Moses, Elijah and Jesus fasted and prayed to prepare themselves for a life's work.

Forty is symbolic of a journey; it is the journey of the catechumens to baptism. They sail over the waters toward the rainbow and march to the promised land of God's reign. Forty is symbolic of a lifetime, the lives of all the baptized. We pattern our lifelong work according to the gospel.

We Journey with the Catechumens

At the beginning of Lent the bishop calls out the names of the catechumens who seek to be baptized at Easter. He writes them in the book of the "elect," the "chosen." God has chosen them, and they have chosen to turn to God. Lent is the 40 days before the baptism of the catechumens. In more and more parishes, the already baptized are able to share the excitement and the struggles of the "elect," and come to rediscover the meaning of baptism in their own lives. During the 40 days, both catechumens and the already baptized journey together to the holy font.

We keep Lent *together*. We turn together, as a parish, as a church of so many colors, ages and ways of life. We put aside our business-as-usual to support each other in prayer, fasting and almsgiving. We turn to God to enlighten us and purify us throughout the lengthening brightness of our holy Lent.

"For now is the acceptable time!
Now is the day of salvation!"

2 Corinthians 6:2

SPECIAL DAYS

Saint Patrick, March 17

(GENESIS 12:1–3)

During Lent Bishop Patrick held up
a shamrock to remind catechumens
that they would soon be baptized in the
name of the Trinity. He transformed
the Celtic May Day bonfire into the new
fire of Easter. Patrick's lenten feastday
is often celebrated as a "festive fast," with
fish and a great bannock bread marked
with the holy cross.

Purim, the full moon before Passover

(ESTHER 9:20–32)

God turns the world upside down. Esther
and Mordechai awaited the destruction of their people, but the destroyer
was destroyed. They mortified themselves
in ashes, but their fast became a feast.
In the reign of God, those who cast
"lots," *purim,* with innocent lives will
have evil recoil on their own heads.

Saint Joseph, March 19

(MATTHEW 1:18–24)

As the earth awakens from its winter's sleep, we remember Joseph, the "dreamer of dreams." Joseph awoke to the dawning of God's reign! Celebrate with a "Joseph's Table" of lenten foods offered to friends and strangers alike. Hymns are sung while money is collected for the poor — prayer, fasting and almsgiving in a single meal.

Annunciation Day, March 25

(LUKE 1:26–38)

On this day the hours of daylight surpass the night. Winter is being conquered. Today is a taste of Easter victory. Since pregnancy without marriage was punishable by death, Mary's yes to the angel was acceptance of death. But in this death the Spirit of life conquered. Mary's mortal body conceived the Immortal One.

Morning Prayer

At daybreak Christians rise to praise God. Among the rushed rituals of every morning, we make time for prayer, perhaps even singing a psalm in the shower. God is glorified with every new day, an image of our passover into glory.

The Sign of the Cross

In the name of the Father
and of the Son
and of the Holy Spirit.

Behold! Now is the acceptable time!
Now is the day of salvation!

Hymn

This song may be sung to any long meter tune, such as "Praise God from whom all blessings flow" or "The glory of these forty days."

Again we keep this solemn fast,
A gift of faith from ages past,
This Lent which binds us lovingly
To faith and hope and charity.

More sparing, therefore, let us make
the words we speak, the food we take,

Our sleep, our laughter, ev'ry sense;
Learn peace through holy penitence.

Psalm 57

Care for me, God, take care of me,
I have nowhere else to hide.
Shadow me with your wings
until all danger passes.

O God, rise high above the heavens!
Spread your glory across the earth!

I have decided, O God,
my decision is firm:
to you I will sing my praise.
Awake, my soul, to song!

Awake, my harp and lyre,
so I can wake up the dawn!
I will lift my voice in praise,
sing of you, Lord, to all nations.
For your love reaches heaven's edge,
your unfailing love, the skies.

PSALM 57:2, 6, 8–11

Daily Scripture

*The daily scripture may be read now or at evening prayer.
See the chart on pages 22 – 23.*

The Song of Zechariah

Praise the Lord, the God of Israel,
who shepherds the people and sets them free.

God raises from David's house
a child with power to save.
Through the holy prophets
God promised in ages past
to save us from enemy hands,
from the grip of all who hate us.

The Lord favored our ancestors
recalling the sacred covenant,
the pledge to our ancestor Abraham,
to free us from our enemies,
so we might worship without fear
and be holy and just all our days.

And you, child, will be called
Prophet of the Most High,
for you will come to prepare
a pathway for the Lord
by teaching the people salvation
through forgiveness of their sin.

Out of God's deepest mercy
a dawn will come from on high,
light for those shadowed by death,
a guide for our feet on the way to peace.

Lord's Prayer

Morning prayer concludes with the praying of the Our Father.

EVENING PRAYER

As night draws near, perhaps during our evening meal, we
praise God for the work of the day now passed. We ask
forgiveness for all we have done wrong. And we ask
protection against the coming darkness, an image of our
passover into death.

Candle Lighting

*A candle may be lit to welcome the evening. When the candle is
burning all begin:*

Jesus Christ is the light of the world!
A light no darkness can overpower!

Hymn

*This song may be sung to any long meter tune, such as
"Praise God from whom all blessings flow" or "The glory of
these forty days."*

O Sun of justice, Jesus Christ,
Dispel the darkness of our hearts,
Till your blest light makes nighttime flee
And brings the joys your day imparts.

Now days of grace with mercy flow.
Touch ev'ry heart with sorrow, Lord.
That turned from sin, renewed by grace,
We may press on toward love's reward.

Behold the happy day shall dawn
When in your light earth blooms anew;
Led back again to life's true way,
May we, forgiv'n, rejoice in you.

*Sometimes incense is burned at evening prayer: The grains
are consumed like the evil of the day passed. The good fragrance
and smoke surround and fill us like the sweet presence of the
Lord. This may be done in silence.*

Psalm 51

Have mercy, tender God,
forget that I defied you.
Wash away my sin,
cleanse me from my guilt.

I know my evil well,
it stares me in the face,
evil done to you alone
before your very eyes.

Creator, reshape my heart,
God, steady my spirit.
Do not cast me aside
stripped of your holy spirit.

Save me, bring back my joy,
support me, strengthen my will.
Help me, stop my tears,
and I will sing your goodness.

PSALM 51:3–6, 12–14, 16

The daily scriptures may be read now. See the tables on pages 22–23.

The Song of Mary

I acclaim the greatness of the Lord,
I delight in God my savior,
who regarded my humble state.
Truly from this day on
all ages will call me blest.

For God, wonderful in power,
has used that strength for me.
Holy the name of the Lord!
whose mercy embraces the faithful,
one generation to the next.

The mighty arm of God
scatters the proud in their conceit,
pulls tyrants from their thrones,
and raises up the humble.
The Lord fills the starving
and lets the rich go hungry.

God rescues lowly Israel,
recalling the promise of mercy,
the promise made to our ancestors,
to Abraham's heirs for ever.

Intercessions and Lord's Prayer

At day's end we offer our petitions to the Father in Jesus'
name. We make intercession for our church, our world,
our parish, our neighbors, our family and friends and
ourselves. During Lent we especially pray for the "elect,"
those catechumens who will be baptized at Easter. We
seal all these prayers with the Our Father.

Sunday Scriptures

Week	Year A: 1996, 1999	Year B: 1997, 2000	Year C: 1998, 2001
1 Lent	Gn 2:7–9; 3:1–7	Gn 9:8–15	Dt 26:4–10
	Rom 5:12–19	1 Pt 3:18–22	Rom 10:8–13
	Mt 4:1–11	Mk 1:12–15	Lk 4:1–13
2 Lent	Gn 12:1–4	Gn 22:1–18	Gn 15:5–18
	2 Tm 1:8–10	Rom 8:31–34	Phil 3:17—4:1
	Mt 17:1–9	Mk 9:2–10	Lk 9:28–36
3 Lent	Ex 17:3–7	Ex 20:1–17	Ex 3:1–15
	Rom 5:1–8	1 Cor 1:22–25	1 Cor 10:1–12
	Jn 4:5–42	Jn 2:13–25	Lk 13:1–9
4 Lent	1 Sm 16:1–13	2 Chr 36:14–23	Jos 5:9–12
	Eph 5:8–14	Eph 2:4–10	2 Cor 5:17–21
	Jn 9:1–41	Jn 3:14–21	Lk 15:1–32
5 Lent	Ez 37:12–14	Jer 31:31–34	Is 43:16–21
	Rom 8:8–11	Heb 5:7–9	Phil 3:8–14
	Jn 11:1–45	Jn 12:20–33	Jn 8:1–11
Passion	Is 50:4–7	Is 50:4–7	Is 50:4–7
	Phil 2:6–11	Phil 2:6–11	Phil 2:6–11
	Mt 27:11–54	Mk 15:1–39	Lk 23:1–49

Weekday Scriptures

Ash Wednesday	Jl 2:12–18 and 2 Cor 5:20—6:2	Mt 6:1–6, 16–18
Thursday	Dt 30:15–20	Lk 9:22–25
Friday	Is 58:1–9	Mt 9:14–15
Saturday	Is 58:9–14	Lk 5:27–32

First Week

Monday	Lv 19:1–2, 11–18	Mt 25:31–46
Tuesday	Is 55:10–11	Mt 6:7–15
Wednesday	Jon 3:1–10	Lk 11:29–32
Thursday	Est C:14–25	Mt 7:7–12 (NAB)
Friday	Ez 18:21–28	Mt 5:20–26
Saturday	Dt 26:16–19	Mt 5:43–48

Second Week

Monday	Dn 9:4–10	Lk 6:36–38
Tuesday	Is 1:10, 16–20	Mt 23:1–12
Wednesday	Jer 18:18–20	Mt 20:17 -28
Thursday	Jer 17:5–10	Lk 16:19–31
Friday	Gn 37:3–4, 12–28	Mt 21:33–46
Saturday	Mi 7:14–20	Lk 15:1–3, 11–32

Third Week

Monday	2 Kgs 5:1–15	Lk 4:24–30
Tuesday	Dn 3:25, 34–43	Mt 18:21–35
Wednesday	Dt 4:1, 5–9	Mt 5:17–19
Thursday	Jer 7:23–28	Lk 11:14–23
Friday	Hos 14:2–10	Mk 12:28–34
Saturday	Hos 6:1–6	Lk 18:9–14

Fourth Week

Monday	Is 65:17–21	Jn 4:43–54
Tuesday	Ez 49:1–9, 12	Jn 5:1–16
Wednesday	Is 49:8–15	Jn 5:17–30
Thursday	Ex 32:7–14	Jn 5:31–47
Friday	Wis 2:1, 12–22	Jn 7:1–30
Saturday	Jer 11:18–20	Jn 7:40–53

Fifth Week

Monday	Dn 13:1–62	Jn 8:1–20
Tuesday	Nm 21:4–9	Jn 8:21–30
Wednesday	Dn 3:14–20, 91–95	Jn 8:31–42
Thursday	Gn 17:3–9	Jn 8:51–59
Friday	Jer 20:10–13	Jn 10:31–42
Saturday	Ez 37:21–28	Jn 11:45–56

Holy Week

Monday	Is 42:1–7	Jn 12:1–11
Tuesday	Is 49:1–6	Jn 13:21–38
Wednesday	Is 50:4–9	Mt 26:14–25

Night Prayer

The night is a time of watchfulness and a time of sleep. It is an image of our passover into eternal rest, our hope for heaven. The last prayer before bed might be prayed kneeling during Lent, standing during Eastertime.

May almighty God give us a restful night and a peaceful death.

Psalm 131

Lord, I am not proud,
holding my head too high,
reaching beyond my grasp.

No, I am calm and tranquil
like a weaned child
resting in its mother's arms:
my whole being at rest.

Let Israel rest in the Lord,
now and for ever.

Song of Simeon

Lord, let your servant
now die in peace,
for you kept your promise.

With my own eyes
I see the salvation
you prepared for all peoples:

a light of revelation for the Gentiles
and glory to your people Israel.

The Sign of the Cross

We end the day as we began, with the sign of the cross:

May the almighty and merciful Lord,
the Father and the Son and the Holy Spirit,
bless and keep us. Amen.

Night Prayer to Mary

The final prayer of the day is traditionally to mother Mary.

(During Lent:)

Hail, holy Queen, Mother of mercy,
our life, our sweetness and our hope!
To you we cry, the children of Eve;
to you we send up our sighs,
mourning and weeping in this land of exile.
Turn, then, most gracious advocate,
your eyes of mercy toward us;
lead us home at last
and show us the blessed fruit of your womb, Jesus:
O clement, O loving, O sweet Virgin Mary!

(During Eastertime:)

Queen of heaven, rejoice, alleluia.
For Christ, your son and Son of God, alleluia,
has risen as he said, alleluia.
Pray to God for us, alleluia.

TRIDUUM
THE THREE DAYS

Triduum means "three days." The Paschal Triduum is the three days, counted sunset to sunset, from Holy Thursday night through Easter Sunday evening. During these days we keep one festival, our Passover, our Easter. We come together with all the people of our parish, with all Christians in every time and place, to fast, pray and keep watch for the Passover of the Lord.

Why Three Days?

For three days Esther fasted and Judith kept vigil, the exiles came home to Jerusalem, and the Hebrews marched to the waters of Marah. For three days darkness afflicted the Egyptians, Hezekiah lay mortally ill, Jonah was entombed in the belly of a fish, and Paul waited in blindness.

On the third day Abraham offered his firstborn son, God came down in fire and wind upon Sinai, the boy Jesus was found in "his Father's house," and the man Jesus "performed the first of his signs at Cana of Galilee." Echoing the words of Hosea, Jesus announced the three-day passover of his death, rest and resurrection.

The Paschal Triduum, the "Three Days of Passover," are for us days of death, rest and resurrection. We march to the waters of baptism. We keep watch for light and for liberation. For three days we climb Mount Moriah, Mount Sinai, Mount Golgotha. Those who were lost are found, and those who were exiled come home.

Why Friday, Saturday and Sunday?

The first day of the Triduum, from Holy Thursday sunset to Good Friday sunset, is the sixth day of creation, when God formed us from clay and breath. In dying the Lord Jesus fell asleep, like Adam, that we might be formed from his own body, like Eve. Jesus completed a new creation. On this day we wash each others' feet in tender humility. We fast as if we were again in paradise. And we come to the holy cross as if it were Eden's tree of life.

The second day of the Triduum, beginning Good Friday sunset, is the sabbath. In burial the Lord Jesus rested, and we rest in him. But this day is also an image of the timelessness before time began. In death the Lord Jesus entered the "formless void," the utter nothingness before creation. On this day we continue our fasting with the anxiety of separated lovers. We keep watch, learning the lessons of restfulness, silence and darkness. We reserve this day, unique in all the year, to do nothing at all.

The third day of the Triduum, beginning Holy Saturday sunset, is the great surprise. Light is kindled in darkness. Order is born from chaos. Life puts death to death. The rainbow appears and the Red Sea opens. The Jordan skips, and Jonah swims with the whale. Daniel curls up with lions, and the three youths play with fire. And a slaughtered lamb rises to become our good shepherd.

That's why we make this night shine like day. We tell our best scriptures and sing our favorite psalms. We witness resurrection in our very midst as the newborn children of God rise from the waters of baptism, are christened with the fragrant oil of confirmation, and are led to partake of eucharist.

As the darkness of this night passes over into dawn, our Paschal Triduum — our three-day Passover — is accomplished and irresistible Easter overwhelms the world.

Prayers

The liturgy of the Triduum, from Holy Thursday evening until Easter Sunday, is a single act of worship. Below are some of the prayers of this liturgy to repeat often throughout the fasting of Good Friday and Holy Saturday and the rejoicing of Easter Sunday.

We should glory in the cross
    of our Lord Jesus Christ for he is our
    salvation, our life and our resurrection.
Through him we are saved and made free.

Where charity and love are found, there is God.

Holy is God! Holy and strong!
Holy immortal One, have mercy on us!

We adore you, O Christ, and we bless you,
    for by your holy cross
    you have redeemed the world.

We worship you, Lord,
we venerate your cross,
we praise your resurrection.
Through the cross you brought joy to the world.

SCRIPTURES

Thursday evening:
Exodus 12:1–8, 11–14
1 Corinthians 11:23–26
John 13:1–15

Friday afternoon:
Isaiah 52:13 — 53:12
Hebrews 4:14–16; 5:7–9
John 18:1—19:42

Saturday evening to Sunday dawn:

Genesis 1:1— 2:2
Genesis 22:1–18
Exodus 14:15 — 15:1
Isaiah 54:5–14
Isaiah 55:1–11
Baruch 3:9–15, 32 — 4:4

Ezekiel 36:16–28
Romans 6:3–11
Matthew 28:1–10,
   or: Mark 16:1–7,
   or: Luke 24:1–12

Also customary to read and ponder during the Triduum are Exodus 5–12 (the ten plagues); Deuteronomy 32 (the Song of Moses); Isaiah 5 (the song of the vineyard); Isaiah 38 (canticle of Hezekiah); Song of Songs 3, 5, 8; Lamentations; Jonah; Hosea 6, 11; Joel; as well as chapters 14–17 of John's gospel and the entire epistle to the Hebrews.

EASTER SUNDAY

The finest breakfast of the year belongs on Easter Sunday. And the entire first week of Eastertime is a joyful pro- longation of this breaking of the fast! Our paschal fast becomes our paschal feast.

Set the table with an Easter candle large enough to burn every day for the next 50 days. Place a fine bowl near the candle. Bring home fire and water from the Vigil to light the candle and fill the bowl.

Easter fare is picnic fare, made in advance of Good Friday so we can keep the Triduum free from work. Chose simple foods with deep meaning for your Easter feast: the unleavened bread of affliction and the yeast-raised bread of life, bitter herbs and spring-green herbs, paschal lamb and fatted calf. Serve something made with milk and honey, from Italian cassata to Russian cheesecake, from Cuban rice pudding to American eggnog. And remember to invite friend and stranger alike to your breakfast. Who knows? Such strangers have been known to set our hearts on fire!

Make the family's cross your tree of life. Decorate it with sprouting branches or even a whole tree, festooned with hollow eggs and bright ribbons. Hang a victory wreath on your front door. Surprise your neighbors with palms, pussywillows and peacock feathers, all symbols of eternal life. Share Easter baskets as a taste of the sweetness of the Lord. Plan an egg hunt, and go searching for signs of springtime's life hidden among winter's death.

At breakfast, with the candle glowing with holy fire and the bowl brimming with holy water, nestle rainbowed eggs in a green bed of sprouted grain. Sprinkle everyone and everything with Easter water. Pass around the eggs, and then crack them against each other while saying: Christ is risen! Christ is truly risen!

EASTERTIME
THE FIFTY DAYS

The Jewish people mark the spring with two great
festivals, *Pesach* and *Shavuot* known to us as Passover and
Pentecost. Pesach comes with the full moon after the
spring equinox. In Israel it falls at the season of the barley
harvest. Shavuot comes 50 days later, at the season of
the wheat harvest. Both are festivals that recall the very
soul of Israel's existence as a people. Pesach renews the
going out from Egypt when the Lord heard the groaning
of the slaves and brought them out with a mighty hand.
Shavuot marks the giving of the law on Sinai, the
covenant between God and every generation of the
Jewish people.

For Christians, these 50 springtime days begin with that Pesach of which Paul wrote: Christ *our Passover* has been sacrificed. And the 50 days end with the story of the Spirit rushing upon the disciples on Shavuot.

The Fifty Days, Our Great Sunday

Fifty days are a seventh of the year, and so we keep our 50-day Eastertime as a long Lord's Day, the "great Sunday." Fifty days are a week of weeks plus a day, a symbol of eternity. And so we keep Eastertime "playing heaven," living as if God's reign has already come. Christians — newly baptized and long baptized — are to live in the wedding feast of heaven and earth, no fasting, no mourning, endlessly singing our Alleluia.

In more and more parishes, Eastertime is not just remembering something that happened long ago. It is Christ dead and risen in our midst. It is the Spirit breathing in us today. For Easter is made present in the neophytes, the newly baptized among us. And it is baptism that tells us what to do with these 50 days.

The Fifty Days, Our Honeymoon

Baptism has its consequences. There is a great mystery to learn and a great mission to begin — like newlyweds beginning their life together. In the *Exsultet* of Easter Eve we sing: "Night truly blest when heaven is wedded to earth." In baptism we are embraced by God and are embracing God. We are married! And Eastertime — all 50 days — is the honeymoon.

How do we keep this honeymoon? How do we make every day of the 50 days a feast of the Spirit? We hike the road of Emmaus and picnic by the Sea of Galilee and climb the Mount of Olives. Eastertime is for zoos and for gardens. Eastertime is for unlocking doors and for unlocking hearts. Eastertime is for fishing and back-packing, for kite-flying and barbecuing — everything that is wholesome, healthy and holy!

Celebrate Eastertime with signs of the risen Spirit. Open your doors in hospitality. Bring the healing peace of Christ to all whose hearts are wintry. Renew your efforts to restore the good earth to the freshness of creation. The risen Spirit of Jesus bids us to spill out into the streets, like the apostles on Pentecost. The good shepherd calls us out to verdant pasture. The wonderful gardener brings us home to paradise.

Special Days

Yom Hashoah, the twelfth day after Passover begins

(Jeremiah 8:18–23)

Soon after the Jewish people keep Passover, the festival of liberation, they remember the Shoah, the destruction of Jews throughout Europe by the Nazis. Perhaps we, too, can begin to remember by accepting our responsibility, and by joining in solidarity with Jews to proclaim, "Never again."

Saint George, April 23

(Revelation 12:7–12)

A dragon held a village hostage until the daughter of the king agreed to become the dragon's dinner. But Saint George slew the dragon and married the princess. Is this only a legend? Whenever we battle against death or despair, it's as if a dragon is slain. Royal funerals become royal weddings! Who knows what Eastertime adventures await?

May Day, May 1

(SONG OF SONGS 2:8–17)

A maypole is the scepter of the May Lord.
He comes to wed his May Lady. It's a
marvelous image, really, the king of
spring chasing away the winter. Jesus is
our May Lord. His scepter is the cross,
and the winter he chases is death. We are
his May Lady. And Eastertime with
maypoles and maywine and maybaskets,
is our honeymoon.

Ascension Day, the fortieth day of Eastertime

(ACTS 1:1–11)

The resurrection of Jesus didn't end on
Easter Sunday. All creation is ascending
into glory. All the universe is becom-
ing divine. Today, with a blare of trumpets
and a vision of angels, we are told to
quit cloud gazing and to start spreading
the good news. Every living thing must
be welcomed to our Easter festival.

Morning Prayer

Every morning is an awakening to Easter, an image of
resurrection. Every breakfast is a feast of the risen Spirit.
We make some time at the beginning of our day
to glorify and thank God for our passover in Christ.

The Sign of the Cross

*During Eastertime it is customary to sign ourselves with water
in remembrance of baptism.*

In the name of the Father
and of the Son
and of the Holy Spirit.

This is the day the Lord has made, alleluia!
Let us rejoice and be glad in it, alleluia!

Hymn

*This song may be sung to its own wonderful melody or to the
melody for "The Strife is O'er."*

Alleluia! Alleluia! Alleluia!

O sons and daughters, let us sing,
The king of heav'n, our glorious king,
O'er death today rose triumphing. Alleluia!

On this most holy day of days
To God your hearts and voices raise
In laud, and jubilee and praise. Alleluia!

Alleluia! Alleluia! Alleluia!

Psalm 30

Lord, how I begged you,
and you, God, healed me.
You pulled me back from the pit,
brought me back from Sheol.

You changed my anguish
into this joyful dance,
pulled off my sackcloth,
gave me bright new robes,
that my life might sing your glory,
never silent in your praise.
For ever I will thank you,
O Lord my God.

PSALM 30:3 – 4, 12 – 13

Daily Scripture

The daily scripture may be read now or at evening prayer. See the chart on pages 46-47.

The Song of Zechariah

Praise the Lord, the God of Israel,
who shepherds the people and sets them free.

God raises from David's house
a child with power to save.
Through the holy prophets
God promised in ages past
to save us from enemy hands,
from the grip of all who hate us.

The Lord favored our ancestors
recalling the sacred covenant,
the pledge to our ancestor Abraham,
to free us from our enemies,
so we might worship without fear
and be holy and just all our days.

And you, child, will be called
Prophet of the Most High,
for you will come to prepare
a pathway for the Lord
by teaching the people salvation
through forgiveness of their sin.

Out of God's deepest mercy
a dawn will come from on high,
light for those shadowed by death,
a guide for our feet on the way to peace.

Lord's Prayer

Morning prayer concludes with the praying of the Our Father.

EVENING PRAYER

Nightfall during Eastertime reminds us of the gospel
accounts of evening meals with the risen Christ.
Whenever we gather by lamplight to break bread in praise
of God, Christ is in our midst.

Candle Lighting

*An Easter candle may be lit to welcome the evening. When the
candle is burning all begin:*

Jesus Christ is the light of the world, alleluia!
A light no darkness can overpower, alleluia!

Hymn

This song may be sung to the tune of "Jesus Christ is ris'n today."

Love's redeeming work is done, Alleluia!
Fought the fight, the battle won. Alleluia!
Death in vain forbids him rise. Alleluia!
Christ has opened paradise. Alleluia!

Soar we now where Christ has led, Alleluia!
Christ the firstborn from the dead. Alleluia!

Made like God, like God we rise, Alleluia!
Ours the cross, the grave, the skies. Alleluia!

Psalm 114

Israel marches out of Egypt,
Jacob leaves an alien people.
Judah becomes a holy place,
Israel, God's domain.

The sea pulls back for them,
the Jordan flees in retreat.
Mountains jump like rams,
hills like lambs in fear.

Why shrink back, O sea?
Jordan, why recoil?
Why shudder, mountains, like rams?
Why quiver, hills, like lambs?

Tremble! earth, before the Lord,
before the God of Jacob,
who turns rock to water,
flint to gushing streams.

Daily Scripture

The daily scriptures may be read now. See the tables on pages 46-47.

The Song of Mary

I acclaim the greatness of the Lord,
I delight in God my savior,
who regarded my humble state.
Truly from this day on
all ages will call me blest.

For God, wonderful in power,
has used that strength for me.
Holy the name of the Lord!
whose mercy embraces the faithful,
one generation to the next.

The mighty arm of God
scatters the proud in their conceit,
pulls tyrants from their thrones,
and raises up the humble.
The Lord fills the starving
and lets the rich go hungry.

God rescues lowly Israel,
recalling the promise of mercy,
the promise made to our ancestors,
to Abraham's heirs for ever.

Intercessions and Lord's Prayer

At day's end we offer our petitions to the Father in Jesus' name. We make intercession for our church, our world, our parish, our neighbors, our family and friends and ourselves. During Eastertime we especially pray for those people who were baptized during the Triduum. We seal all these prayers with the Our Father.

Sunday Scriptures

Week	Cycle A: 1996, 1999	Cycle B: 1197, 2000	Cycle C: 1998, 2001
Easter	Acts 10:34–43 Col 3:1–4 Jn 20:1–9	Acts 10:34–43 Col 3:1–4 Jn 20:1–9	Acts 10:34–43 Col 3:1–4 Jn 20:1–9
2 Easter	Acts 2:42–47 1 Pt 1:3–9 Jn 20:19–31	Acts 4:32–35 1 Jn 5:1–6 Jn 20:19–31	Acts 5:12–16 Rv 1:9–19 Jn 20:19–31
3 Easter	Acts 2:14–28 1 Pt 1:17–21 Lk 24:13–35	Acts 3:13–19 1 Jn 2:1–5 Lk 24:35–48	Acts 5:27–41 Rv 5:11–14 Jn 21:1–19
4 Easter	Acts 2:14, 36–41 1 Pt 2:20–25 Jn 10:1–10	Acts 4:8–12 1 Jn 3:1–2 Jn 10:11–18	Acts 13:14, 43–52 Rv 7:9, 14–17 Jn 10:27–30
5 Easter	Acts 6:1–7 1 Pt 2:4–9 Jn 14:1–12	Acts 9:26–31 1 Jn 3:18–24 Jn 15:1–8	Acts 14:21–27 Rv 21:1–5 Jn 13:31–35
6 Easter	Acts 8:5–17 Pt 3:15–18 Jn 14:15–21	Acts 10:25–48 1 Jn 4:7–10 Jn 15:9–17	Acts 15:1–2, 22–29 Rv 21:10–23 Jn 14:23–29
7 Easter	Acts 1:12–14 Pt 4:13–16 Jn 17:1–11	Acts 1:15–26 1 Jn 4:11–16 Jn 17:11–19	Acts 7:55–60 Rv 29:12–20 Jn 17:20–26
Pentecost	Acts 2:1–11 1 Cor 12:3–13 Jn 20:19–23	Acts 2:1–11 1 Cor 12:3–13 Jn 20:19–23	Acts 2:1–11 1 Cor 12:3–13 Jn 20:19–23

Weekday Scriptures

First Week
Easter Monday	Acts 2:14, 22 – 33	Mt 28:8 –15
Easter Tuesday	Acts 2:36 – 41	Jn 20:11–18
Easter Wednesday	Acts 3:1–10	Lk 24:13 – 35
Easter Thursday	Acts 3:11– 26	Lk 24:35 – 48
Easter Friday	Acts 4:1–12	Jn 21:1–14
Easter Saturday	Acts 4:13 – 21	Mark 16:9 –15

Second Week
Monday	Acts 4:23 – 31	Jn 3:1– 8
Tuesday	Acts 4:39 – 37	Jn 3:7–15
Wednesday	Acts 5:17– 26	Jn 3:16 – 21
Thursday	Acts 5:27– 33	Jn 3:31– 36
Friday	Acts 5:34 – 42	Jn 6:1–15
Saturday	Acts 6:1–7	Jn 6:16 – 21

Third Week
Monday	Acts 6:8 –15	Jn 6:22 – 29
Tuesday	Acts 7:51—8:1	Jn 6:30 – 35
Wednesday	Acts 8:1– 8	Jn 6:35 – 40
Thursday	Acts 8:26 – 40	Jn 6:44 – 51
Friday	Acts 9:1– 20	Jn 6:52 – 59
Saturday	Acts 9:31– 42	Jn 6:60 – 69

Fourth Week
Monday	Acts 11:1–18	Jn 10:1–10
Tuesday	Acts 11:19 – 26	Jn 10:22 – 30
Wednesday	Acts 12:24—13:5	Jn 12:44 – 50
Thursday	Acts 13:13 – 25	Jn 13:16 – 20
Friday	Acts 13:26 – 33	Jn 14:1– 6
Saturday	Acts 13:44 – 52	Jn 14:7–14

Fifth Week

Monday	Acts 14:15–18	Jn 14:21–26
Tuesday	Acts 14:19–28	Jn 14:27–31
Wednesday	Acts 15:1–6	Jn 15:1–8
Thursday	Acts 15:7–21	Jn 15:9–11
Friday	Acts 15:22–31	Jn 15:12–17
Saturday	Acts 16:1–10	Jn 15:18–21

Sixth Week

Monday	Acts 16:11–15	Jn 15:26—16:4
Tuesday	Acts 16:22–34	Jn 16:5–11
Wednesday	Acts 17:15, 22—18:1	Jn 16:12–15
Thursday	Acts 1:1–11	Mt 28:16–20
Friday	Acts 18:9–18	Jn 16:20–23
Saturday	Acts 18:23–28	Jn 16:23–28

Seventh Week

Monday	Acts 19:1–8	Jn 16:29–33
Tuesday	Acts 20:17–27	Jn 17:1–11
Wednesday	Acts 20:28–38	Jn 17:11–19
Thursday	Acts 22:30; 23:6–11	Jn 17:20–26
Friday	Acts 25:13–21	Jn 21:15–19
Saturday morning	Acts 28:16–20,	Jn 21:20–25, 30–31
Pentecost Vigil	Gn 11:l–9;	Jn 7:37–39
	Ex 19:3–8, 16–20; Ez 37:1–14; Jl 3:15	

On weekdays during Eastertime you may read Genesis 6–9 (the great flood), Genesis 11 (the tower of Babel), Exodus 16–19 (the journey to Sinai), Jeremiah 31 (the end of exile), Daniel 3 (the fiery furnace), Daniel 14 (the dragon and the lions' den), as well as the books of Jonah, Judith, Song of Songs, 1 Peter, 1 John and Revelation.

PENTECOST

The springtime has passed over into summer. What was barren burgeons with green. What was chilled simmers with heat. The sun rises to its zenith as daytime stretches into endless twilight. Our windows open. Our doors unlock. The sprouting grain bears its fiftyfold fruit. Our Easter is complete.

So we tell stories of fulfillment and completion. We tell of open doors and open hearts. We tell of the Spirit, who broods like a dove, windswept over the waters.

Pentecost is Easter grown up. Eggs become birds (paracletes!), blossoms become first fruits and liberty becomes law. These things demand celebration. For Easter without Pentecost is like a promise not kept, or a child unable to grow. So with Spirit-inspired joy we celebrate with all the signs of spring-turned-summer, with windsocks and wines, peonies and perfumes, kites and candles, with asparagus soufflé and rhubarb pie, with signs of growth accomplished and promises kept.

Today Lent, Triduum and Eastertime are done. The journey we began so long ago in ashes is finished in fire.